The Baton Rouge Bus Boycott

The Baton Rouge Bus Boycott:

The Mark That Could Not Be Erased

ROBIN WHITE CLARK

Copyright © 2020 Robin White Clark.

All rights reserved. No part of this publication may be reproduced, distributed, or transmitted in any form or by any means, including photocopying, recording, or other electronic or mechanical methods, without the prior written permission of the publisher, except in the case of brief quotations embodied in critical reviews and certain other noncommercial uses permitted by copyright law. For permission requests, write to the publisher, addressed "Attention: Permissions Coordinator," at the address below.

ISBN: 978-1-7341206-0-8 (Paperback)

ASIN: B084V18M99 (eBook)

ISBN: 978-1-7341206-2-2 (Coloring Book)

Library of Congress Control Number: 2020901531

Front cover design by Robin White Clark.
Front cover image by Russell L. Kelly Sr.
Book design by Robin White Clark.

Printed in the United States of America.

First printing edition, 2020.

Rhema Enterprises LLC
12637 King James Avenue
Baton Rouge, LA 70810-3226

Email: RobinWhiteClark@gmail.com

Photo Credits: The White Family (Personal Collections), Renard A. Smith (p. 12 - bottom), and Russell L. Kelly Sr. (p. 17 - bottom)

Dedication

For the countless hidden figures and unsung heroes
in our Black American history, tell the story and
preserve the history for the children.

Acknowledgement

My hope is that this poetic story and pictures of events help your understanding of the role of the Baton Rouge Bus Boycott in American History. Writing poetry and collecting this information was not an easy endeavor. The family and friends who shared their stories with me over the years are now between the ages of 60 and 100 years old. Others have died and their words are whispers in my ears. I want to honor their oral history. When possible, I have confirmed their thoughts and memories with known facts. Take special note of the Author's Comments written in the Index of Photos. I hope that there are no errors. It is my prayer that I have accurately contributed to the preservation of America's history, Baton Rouge's history, and my family's legacy.

Foreword

Many people think that the Civil Rights Movement began with the Montgomery Boycott in 1955. The reality is that before there was a bus boycott in Montgomery, there was the Baton Rouge Bus Boycott in 1953. The Baton Rouge Boycott was used by Rev. Martin Luther King as the "blueprint" or foundation for the Montgomery Boycott. America's *Civil Rights Struggle* began in Jamestown, VA when the first enslaved Africans were brought on a Dutch ship in 1619. Following Jamestown, there was slavery, Reconstruction and Redemption, the Jim Crow era, and then the *Modern Civil Rights Movement*.

Equally important to you should be your family's history. My sister has chosen to use family pictures and pictures from other sources to add value and help interpret her creative poetic expression of the Baton Rouge Bus Boycott. Some of our best times have been talking to family members. You are encouraged to research and confirm your family's oral history by examining family photographs, looking at genealogy records in libraries/websites, and reviewing conveyance and succession/estate records in Clerk of Court offices.

Make the time to do the work to transfer your family's oral history into an indelible impression in history. By doing so, you will pay homage to your ancestors and **leave a mark that could not be erased!**

(Judge) Trudy M. White

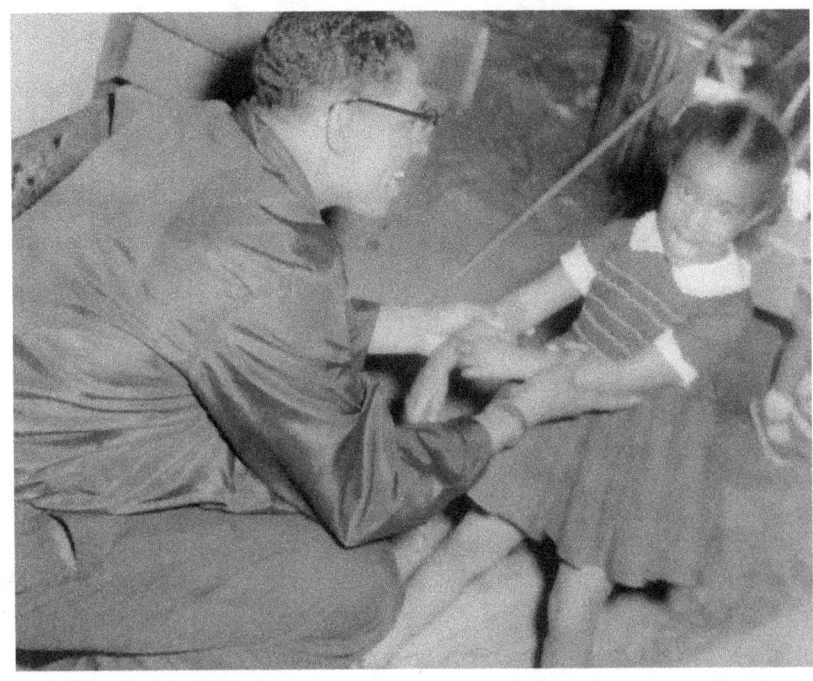

Table of Contents

The Baton Rouge Bus Boycott (The Picture Story) 1

Hidden Figures and Unsung Heroes 21

    Acie J. Belton 22

    Rev. E. Doyle Billoups 23

    Dr. George Butler 24

    Judge Lewis S. Doherty III 25

    Hazel Lucille Johnson Freeman 26

    Rev. T. J. Jemison 27

    Attorney Johnnie A. Jones Sr 28

    Sadie Roberts-Joseph 29

    Willis V. Reed Sr 30

    Raymond Scott 31

    T. Roosevelt Smith Sr 32

    Horatio C. Thompson 33

    Martha White 34

    Adolph Wiggins Sr 35

The Baton Rouge Bus Boycott (The Poem) 36

Index of Photos 38

ROBIN WHITE CLARK

The Baton Rouge Bus Boycott:
The Mark That Could Not Be Erased

(The Picture Story)

ROBIN WHITE CLARK

ROBIN WHITE CLARK

Oil sausage sandwiches
Rich and greasy to the mouth
It was different in Baton Rouge
Very different in the South

Summer heat with no air conditioning
Shotgun houses and church fans
Black nannies, maids and housekeepers
And jobs with manual labor demands

Black children stopped drowning
In the Mississippi River and streams
For swimming at Brooks Park
Became the ultimate of dreams

Eating Grandmother Gert's tea cakes
While reading books galore
Black kids could enjoy them both
On the Carver Library floor

Tasting Chicken Shack chicken
Spicy and so delicious, we agree
This was the summer
It was June of 1953

It was a time of separation
A time of segregation
Blacks needed to stay in their place
Remain with their own ethnic persuasion

Getting around Baton Rouge
In 93 to 100-degree sweltering heat
Meant riding the city bus, using a car
Or just walking down the street

Not many Blacks had cars
Black-owned buses were already banned
Forced detours around White neighborhoods
Always interrupted Black traveling plans

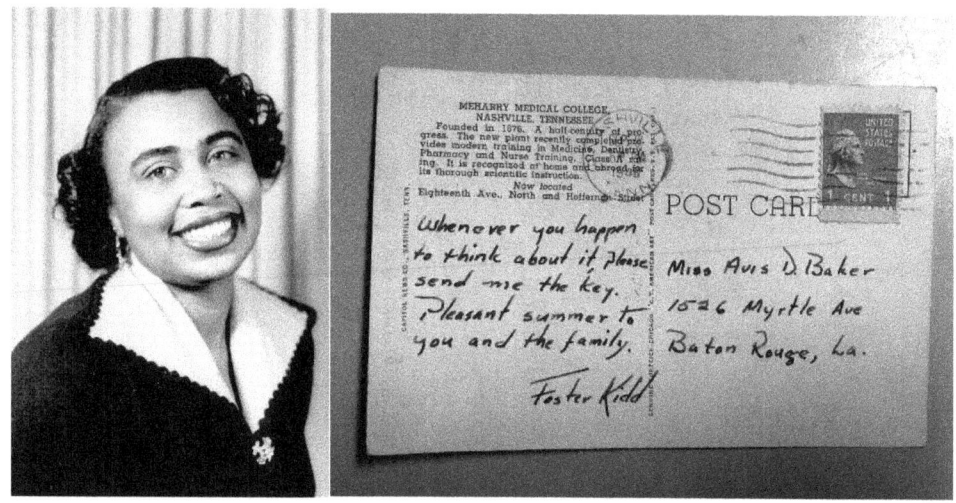

A postage stamp was only 3 cents
When the White-owned city bus fare goes up
From 10 cents to 15 cents
That's a 50% markup!

Ordinance 222 was ruled illegal
First-come, first-served wouldn't be the law
White bus drivers wouldn't hear of it
Jim Crow was all that the South saw

Just pay that new bus fare
And sit or stand without a fuss
If Black, simply make sure
You sit behind the Whites on the bus

So even when paying full fare
Blacks couldn't always sit and ride
Except when riding through Black neighborhoods
Could they sit down inside

The first two seats, reserved for Whites
Then behind the sign is for the Blacks
Even if there were empty White seats
Just stand up while being Black in the back

Of course, White bus drivers
Truly convinced of their position
Demanded segregated obedience
For this was their Southern tradition

Obedience to the White bus drivers
Was a necessity to ride
As a Black patron on the city bus
All regrets you must hide

So, on June 18th in 1953
The Baton Rouge Bus Boycott began
Rarely a bus did Blacks ride
They didn't sit and they didn't stand

A coalition was forming
And the mass boycott was led
By Rev. T. J. Jemison and Raymond Scott
A free ride network instead

Coordinated through churches
And mass meetings at McKinley High
Collecting money for gas and drivers
Deciding who would walk and who would ride

Afternoon meetings were held
And as the crowds did grow
Memorial Stadium became the new place
For the school did overflow

There are others who contributed
To the cause of this civil event
Like Dr. George Butler or Willis Reed
And T. Roosevelt Smith

Acie Belton and Pastor Billoups
Were instrumental in this fight
Adolph Wiggins Sr. was also there
Committed to doing that which was right

Free rides like with Desselle's Insurance
Uniting Negroes in downtown
To gather together by the Old State Capitol
And just to make it around

To travel to business
To travel to work
They were banding together
Whatever it was worth

What a shock took place
When the White bus drivers realized
That 80% of their paycheck
Was because of Blacks riding inside

With 20% of bus riders left
Bus drivers changed their sentiment
That's a $1500 loss or more
Impacting the company's P & L Statement

With a daily loss that great
It was a desperate scramble to appease
Bankruptcy was certain
Within days, guaranteed

EMERGENCY ORDINANCE 251

Amending Title 10, Chapter 2 of the Baton Rouge City Code of 1951 by amending Section 118, "Seating of Passengers"

(1) Separation of Races in Buses: White passengers shall take seats from the front end of the bus and all Negro passengers boarding shall take seats from the back of the bus.

(2) Reservation of Seats: No White person shall occupy the long rear seat. No Negro passenger shall occupy the two front seats facing the aisle.

(3) No passengers of different races shall occupy the same seat.

Negotiations ensued
With the City Council and leaders of Blacks
Ordinance 251 was adopted
From June 24th, here are the facts

Still Blacks could not sit
In front of someone who was White
Or on the same row with them
In the Deep South that wasn't right

The two front sideway seats
Were exclusively for Whites
The wide rear seat
Was for Blacks (either day or night)

As Whites would board buses
From the front they would sit
As the Blacks would arrive
From the back they would drift

The compromise was agreed upon
Now all bus passengers who loaded
Knew middle seats were free for all
With only three seats color coded

The Baton Rouge Bus Boycott had ended
Establishing both unity and faith
It awakened the Civil Rights Movement
And a way to peacefully demonstrate

So, as we reflect
And as we recall
We shall remain vigilant
We will stand tall

But at times we will sit
On a bench by the road
To garner our thoughts
And redistribute our load

Let us not erase
What others have done and bring
But keep them in remembrance
While we Let Freedom Ring

When Rosa sat still
When Martin had a dream to chase
The Baton Rouge Bus Boycott
Was already the mark that could not be erased

Hidden Figures and Unsung Heroes

Acie J. Belton

Rev. E. Doyle Billoups

Dr. George Butler

Judge Lewis S. Doherty III

Hazel Lucille Johnson Freeman

Rev. T. J. Jemison

Attorney Johnnie A. Jones Sr.

Sadie Roberts-Joseph

Willis V. Reed Sr.

Raymond Scott

T. Roosevelt Smith Sr.

Horatio C. Thompson

Martha White

Adolph Wiggins Sr.

Acie J. Belton

By Robin White Clark

Copyright 2020

Born January in the year 1916
An individual both warm and kind
And a valuable community spokesman
With the heart of the Black community in mind

An early civil rights leader
And a veteran of World War II
A devoted and fine refinery worker
Who always promoted voting in elections too

For he was the founder and president
Of the Second Ward Voters League
And raising political consciousness
The likes of which you have not seen

Organized F.O.C.U.S.
To secure public jobs for Blacks
Included Scotlandville in the city
Through a strategic legal attack

A belief in political engagement
Was always critical it seems
The collaboration during the Baton Rouge Bus Boycott
Would have everlasting economic means

Access to jobs and economic freedom
Fair treatment and true rights is what was meant
No Blacks in Baton Rouge should settle
But worked to overcome disenfranchisement

Rev. E. Doyle Billoups

By Robin White Clark

Copyright 2020

From the parish of West Baton Rouge
In a little town, there still
Is where he was born
The place is called Lukeville

He grew and he grew
For many a year or two
Until he heard from God
What He wanted him to do

He answered the call
And did not procrastinate
At New St. John he became pastor
The year was 1928

The membership grew
From each message he would preach
The congregation was blessed
By every word he did teach

He was certainly a trustee
Of God's holy book
But he committed other time
With the leadership it took

With his wife
Always at his side
Their children were raised
With sincere civil rights pride

He was Vice President-At-Large
Of the National Baptist Convention
He was the sitting president too
Of something I must mention

The LA Missionary Baptist State Convention
Had a focused and singular mission
To preach, teach, and heal
And to fulfill the Great Commission

Dr. George A. Butler

By Robin White Clark

Copyright 2020

Despite being one of 13 children
He was taught to excel
One in an impoverished family
Headed by a sharecropper as well

Born around 1895
Near the turn of the century, they would say
Made a living in South Baton Rouge
And that's where he wanted to stay

His brother Leo and he opened
An imposing block-long place
A location for Black-owned businesses
With a medical office space

With his own practice downstairs
In the brand-new Butler Building core
He was a Black pharmacist
Located inside of the Ideal Drug Store

With his wife, Constance ("Tante")
As the postmaster next door
Entrepreneurialism was alive
From the roof to the bottom floor

The impact of segregation
Created a kind of gloom
So, he decorated with palm trees
In a place called the Blue Room

For having medical care
Was his caring solution
Being a pharmacist for Blacks
Was his personal contribution

Judge Lewis S. Doherty III

By Robin White Clark

Copyright 2020

Born in 1926
To Lewis and Olive, it seems
Proud of his heritage and family
A picture of sweet dreams

A man of fierce integrity
And equality for all
He studied at LSU
That's until the US Navy called

When returning back to school
He completed his Bachelor of Arts degree
On LSU's campus
He pledged Kappa Alpha Fraternity

With a passion for justice
It made sense for him to enter
And finish a new degree
At the Paul M. Hebert Law Center

He practiced the law
And was a man of deep faith
Seated on the Baton Rouge City Council
When the bus boycott was the debate

His actions were always consistent
With the values he felt and thought
Never featured as a civil rights advocate
But admired for the battles he fought

Belief in the equality of races
Was his fervent petition
And settling the 1953 bus boycott
Included his hallmark decision

Hazel Lucille Johnson Freeman

By Robin White Clark

Copyright 2020

First born of 9 siblings
Attended McKinley High School's class
Graduated with honors
A Bachelors in Education she did amass

With grace she framed a vision
To fortify her profession
She attended Columbia University Teachers College
With a Master's degree as her confession

As Supervisor of Child Welfare and Attendance
The East Baton Rouge Parish School System would agree
Her fortitude and charm were unmistaken
As a member of the L.E.A., N.E.A., and D.S.T.

With warmth and a caring countenance
And even as a community volunteer
Her mark of influence and legacy
Shall not be soon to disappear

The founder of the Community Assoc. for the Welfare of School Children
Her role in education was her profession
But do not forget her significant role
In support of the bus boycott against segregation

As a member of Mount Zion Baptist Church
And Secretary to Rev. Gardner C. Taylor
Her political activism with Jemison and Scott
Would support the bus boycott with favor

Rev. T. J. Jemison

By Robin White Clark

Copyright 2020

In Selma, Alabama he was born
During August of 1918
To the union of David and Henrietta
Into a minister's household it seems

At Alabama State he studied
And earned a Bachelor's of Science degree
Then at Virginia Union he would continue
To secure his Masters of Divinity

He organized the first local chapter of the NAACP
Moved to South Baton Rouge after that
Pastored at Mount Zion Baptist Church
And found segregation to be a fact

Although President of the National Baptist Convention
With a membership of over six million strong
The support of desegregation would be the goal
The Baton Rouge Bus Boycott shouldn't take too long

When Martha failed to sit where told
It created a terrible fuss
Then she and two others
Needed assistance on the bus

Jemison, Scott, and Freeman
Arrived on the scene
They knew what had happened
And discerned what it would mean

It was this confrontation that started
What would mean a whole lot
This was the proverbial tipping point
For the Baton Rouge Bus Boycott

Attorney Johnnie A. Jones Sr.

By Robin White Clark

Copyright 2020

He picked cotton in the fields
And hated that sight every day
The son of lease croppers
Shouldn't have to grow up that way

Near the city of St. Francisville
In a schoolhouse with two-rooms
Inspired in 5th grade
His future in law soon blooms

He attended Southern University
Where he learned about the law
As warrant officer in the U.S. Army
He forgot the segregation he saw

For years in World War II
He prepared for D-Day
Now returning to the south
He found segregation the same way

With shrapnel in his neck
He traveled to seek some care
The police knocked him to the ground
And kicked him everywhere

Segregation was a tall order
And it has a very deep root
But he'll be the lawyer
For the Baton Rouge Bus Boycott lawsuit

Sadie Roberts-Joseph

By Robin White Clark

Copyright 2020

Native of Fort Adams, Mississippi
Living life as a resident of Baton Rouge
Establisher of Community Against Drugs and Violence
An advocate of civil rights views

A stunningly colorful beauty
Both inside her heart and out
An incredible example to the world
And a mother who was simply devout

A founder and master teacher
An establisher to educate
The Odell S. Williams Museum
Would fill with warmth those who would congregate

Independent and determined
And tirelessly inquisitive
She carried herself with great poise
With a smile continuously affective

A sophisticated community icon
Locally known and loved
State renown in her own right
Nationally declared and beloved

Loving one another
Letting peace and unity prevail
Acknowledging past injustices
Living life now beyond the veil

Willis V. Reed Sr.

By Robin White Clark

Copyright 2020

Born in October
It was the 14th in 1913
Served in the WWII army
Decorated with 3 battle stars of means

Honorably discharged
After serving our country
Now committed to the cause of justice
For the Baton Rouge community

Willis V. Reed Sr.
Operated the newspaper of the day
It was he who could spread the written word
He was Facebook in a way

Founder of the First Ward Voters League
Newspaper owner of the Baton Rouge Post
A principle in the Baton Rouge Bus Boycott
Notifying Blacks by radio he could boast

It was he who went to WLCS radio
With T. J. Jemison, I believe
That the bus boycott would happen
The next day it would proceed

It happened just like this
On June 20, 1953
Free rides were being coordinated
It was a defining moment in our history

Raymond Scott

By Robin White Clark

Copyright 2020

He was the Secretary
Of the United Defense League
And was there for his community
To help Blacks succeed

Scott, the Tailor
As he was called
Was much more than that
As we recall

The only place
Where Blacks could go
To get dressed up
In a tuxedo or so

He lived next door
To his tailor shop
And across the street
From Delpit's Chicken stop

He was a silent soldier
Who would laugh and smile
Would measure you for a coat
And give you gas for a mile

Black nannies had to travel
For they were employed by Whites
He provided taxis and cars
From daytime to nights

He funded and fueled
A community of Blacks
With gas and transportation
While making a historic impact

ROBIN WHITE CLARK

T. Roosevelt Smith Sr.

By Robin White Clark

Copyright 2020

He was born in a logging town
That a hurricane washed away
Ruddock is a ghost town
That's what they call it today

He graduated from high school
And sold peanuts all around
The money was for his family
On South Baton Rouge streets, he could be found

He was gainfully employed
As a laborer at Standard Oil
In spite of discrimination
From responsibility he did not recoil

President of the Colored Union
The title he held for many years
Instrumental in desegregation
With his blood, sweat, and tears

Prexy for short
Was his endearing nickname
He was the Executive Chairman of the Board
A prominent leader, just the same

The United Defense League
Spearheaded the legal demand
It was June of 1953
When the Baton Rouge Bus Boycott began

Horatio C. Thompson

By Robin White Clark

Copyright 2020

Born in New Orleans
On Southern's yard, he went to school
Out of his college dorm room
Selling drug store items was his rule

Started a taxi service
For dignitaries of the Jaguar nation
This seed led to another
Where he owned gas franchise stations

As a resident of Baton Rouge
He married Jewell, his precious wife
They had two lovely daughters
Phyllis and Paula were blessings in their life

Member of Kappa Alpha Psi
Honored with Laurel Wealth
Founder of St. Michael's Episcopal Church
Vital to the Black community's health

Honored as a man of distinction
And an iconic elder statesman
Known as a civil rights advocate
And a perfectly sound gentleman

A leader with integrity
Owner of gas service stations
He was a Black businessman in the city
Joining the fight for integration

It was during the bus boycott
That a strategy would come up
Using the Free Ride System
Could support the effort enough

He sold gasoline to boycott drivers
At the cost that he paid
Personally fueling the cause
By the sacrifice he willingly made

Martha White

By Robin White Clark

Copyright 2020

She worked as a housekeeper
Many days of her young life
And bought her very own home
With the wages from days and night

Working on her feet
Was a typical employee position
Enduring exhausting bus rides
Was a part of her working condition

At 23 years of age
She walked many miles to ride
The Baton Rouge city bus
And often stood up inside

In June 1953
On the morning she would ride
The segregated public bus
With limited seats inside

The only seat left
Was in the White Only section she spied
She was tired and took the seat
When prompted to get up, she simply complied

Way from the back
A mockery of laughter they cried
She heard and sat back down
And was almost arrested, but denied

The city bus was stopped
And the White bus driver called
Then all of the police arrived
Even the Bus Commissioner was appalled

Intervention saved her from jail
She vowed she'd never ride on a bus
But now there was a problem
And a tremendous ruckus

The radio announcement was
For all Blacks to meet at McKinley High
The attendance was so vast
That everyone could not fit inside

The next location to meet
Would be Memorial Stadium, you see
To discuss the appropriate process
Then Ordinance 222 became the decree

Blacks came together
And were united in South Baton Rouge
The Baton Rouge Bus Boycott of 1953
Would make historic civil rights news

Adolph Wiggins Sr.

By Robin White Clark

Copyright 2020

He was a devout Catholic
At St. Joseph's Cathedral
Very close to his wife
And especially blessed by the Lord

He never looked down on others
But believed in equality for all
Took great pleasure in helping
The elderly at nursing halls

An outstanding member
Who helped acquire the place
Of Alpha Phi Alpha Fraternity's
North Foster gathering space

He was brother to Inez Chrisentery
And had a great since of humor
He enjoyed traveling the country
At least, that's the rumor

He and his wife had kids
They were Adolph Jr. and Janie
Caring for them and the community at large
Could often be quite zany

Did not seek out recognition
Even when life could be very hard
He remained as Asst. Superintendent
At the Post Office on Florida Boulevard

Adolph was easy to admire
As a handsome dear man
Focusing on Black awareness
And being a great humanitarian

The Baton Rouge Bus Boycott: The Mark That Could Not Be Erased
By Robin White Clark

Oil sausage sandwiches
Rich and greasy to the mouth
It was different in Baton Rouge
Very different in the South

Summer heat with no air conditioning
Shotgun houses and church fans
Black nannies, maids and housekeepers
And jobs with manual labor demands

Black children stopped drowning
In the Mississippi River and streams
For swimming at Brooks Park
Became the ultimate of dreams

Eating Grandmother Gert's tea cakes
While reading books galore
Black kids could enjoy them both
On the Carver Library floor

Tasting Chicken Shack chicken
Spicy and so delicious, we agree
This was the summer
It was June of 1953

It was a time of separation
A time of segregation
Blacks needed to stay in their place
Remain with their own ethnic persuasion

Getting around Baton Rouge
In 93 to 100-degree sweltering heat
Meant riding the city bus, using a car
Or just walking down the street

Not many Blacks had cars
Black-owned buses were already banned
Forced detours around White neighborhoods
Always interrupted Black traveling plans

A postage stamp was only 3 cents
When the White-owned city bus fare goes up
From 10 cents to 15 cents
That's a 50% markup!

Ordinance 222 was ruled illegal
First-come, first-served wouldn't be the law
White bus drivers wouldn't hear of it
Jim Crow was all that the South saw

Just pay that new bus fare
And sit or stand without a fuss
If Black, simply make sure
You sit behind the Whites on the bus

So even when paying full fare
Blacks couldn't always sit and ride
Except when riding through Black neighborhoods
Could they sit down inside

The first two seats, reserved for Whites
Then behind the sign is for the Blacks
Even if there were empty White seats
Just stand up while being Black in the back

Of course, White bus drivers
Truly convinced of their position
Demanded segregated obedience
For this was their Southern tradition

Obedience to the White bus drivers
Was a necessity to ride
As a Black patron on the city bus
All regrets you must hide

So, on June 18th in 1953
The Baton Rouge Bus Boycott began
Rarely a bus did Blacks ride
They didn't sit and they didn't stand

A coalition was forming
And the mass boycott was led
By Rev. T. J. Jemison and Raymond Scott
A free ride network instead

Coordinated through churches
And mass meetings at McKinley High
Collecting money for gas and drivers
Deciding who would walk and who would ride

The Baton Rouge Bus Boycott: The Mark That Could Not Be Erased
By Robin White Clark

Afternoon meetings were held
And as the crowds did grow
Memorial Stadium became the new place
For the school did overflow

There are others who contributed
To the cause of this civil event
Like Dr. George Butler or Willis Reed
And T. Roosevelt Smith

Acie Belton and Pastor Billoups
Were instrumental in this fight
Adolph Wiggins Sr. was also there
Committed to doing that which was right

Free rides like with Desselle's Insurance
Uniting Negroes in downtown
To gather together by the Old State Capitol
And just to make it around

To travel to business
To travel to work
They were banding together
Whatever it was worth

What a shock took place
When the White bus drivers realized
That 80% of their paycheck
Was because of Blacks riding inside

With 20% of bus riders left
Bus drivers changed their sentiment
That's a $1500 loss or more
Impacting the company's P & L Statement

With a daily loss that great
It was a desperate scramble to appease
Bankruptcy was certain
Within days, guaranteed

Negotiations ensued
With the City Council and leaders of Blacks
Ordinance 251 was adopted
From June 24th, here are the facts

Still Blacks could not sit
In front of someone who was White
Or on the same row with them
In the Deep South that wasn't right

The two front sideway seats
Were exclusively for Whites
The wide rear seat
Was for Blacks (either day or night)

As Whites would board buses
From the front they would sit
As the Blacks would arrive
From the back they would drift

The compromise was agreed upon
Now all bus passengers who loaded
Knew middle seats were free for all
With only three seats color coded

The Baton Rouge Bus Boycott had ended
Establishing both unity and faith
It awakened the Civil Rights Movement
And a way to peacefully demonstrate

So, as we reflect
And as we recall
We shall remain vigilant
We will stand tall

But at times we will sit
On a bench by the road
To garner our thoughts
And redistribute our load

Let us not erase
What others have done and bring
But keep them in remembrance
While we Let Freedom Ring

When Rosa sat still
When Martin had a dream to chase
The Baton Rouge Bus Boycott
Was already the mark that could not be erased

Index of Photos

Author's Comments

Dedication Page

On the left is Kirkland Collier and on the right is me, Robin White Clark. We are investigating a tricycle in the yard of a family member. We loved playing and being at "Aunt Doon's" and "Uncle Wilbert's house." As a teacher, I feel that I was (even then) trying to share information. This is my favorite childhood photo.

Foreword Page

This is a photo of (Judge) Trudy M. White with Wilbert White, Jr. They are at the house of Wilbert and Louise "Aunt Doon" DeCuir White near McKinley Middle Magnet School. The house was located in South Baton Rouge on a high hill at the corner of Fig Street and 13th Street.

Page 3 Oil sausage sandwiches

Oil sausage sandwiches were a poor man's lunch back in the 1950's. It was literally a sandwich made with two slices of white bread, canned Vienna-type sausage cut in half lengthwise, sweet or sour pickles, and mayonnaise. Often it was accompanied by a sweet dessert called stage plank. Stage plank was a long rectangular gingerbread type cookie with pink and white icing on it. My grandmother made oil sausage sandwiches for my lunch in elementary school. It is one of my fondest memories of her love.

Page 3 Shotgun House

A shotgun house was usually a wooden framed house with one entrance in the front and one exit in the back. There might be a clear view from the front door though the house to the back door. The area was about 800 to 1,000 square feet with probably 1 bedroom, 1 bathroom, 1 kitchen and 1 living room. Today it would be called a tiny house. This design supported natural ventilation for cooling and heating. Unfortunately, natural ventilation wasn't effective for extreme heat or cold. In the photo (left to right) are Avis Baker-White (my mom), Ezeria Blanchard White (my paternal grandmother), and Avery Blanchard (my paternal great-uncle and Ezeria's brother). The children are Ezeria's grandchildren, Ronald Davidson (left) and his brother, Arthur Turner Davidson.

Page 4 Brooks Park Pool Bldg. and Shawn Clark at the pool

Rev. W. K. Brooks, the United Negro Recreation Association, and a host of good people in South Baton Rouge came together to build the first Negro swimming pool in a time when Black children were drowning in unsafe waters. Swimming lessons and water safety training became a priority at Brooks Park pool. The site was chosen and built next to the McKinley Middle School which educated the all Black population in South Baton Rouge over two shifts. One shift would go to school and the other shift would be entertained at Brooks Park and the pool. Trust and the tight-knit community took care of the children all day. The original pool has been reduced to a much smaller footprint. Originally, there was a wading pool too. It has since been covered over or destroyed. In its place is an outdoor pavilion or gazebo with tables.

It was important to me that my son, Shawn J. Clark, (pictured here) spend time swimming at Brooks Park (aka City Brooks Park). I wanted him to have some connection to this pool and help keep our legacy alive. This pool photo was taken in June of 2006. The photo of the building was taken in January of 2020.

THE BATON ROUGE BUS BOYCOTT

Page 4 Carver Branch Library

The South Baton Rouge neighborhood of predominantly Black families was a self-sufficient community. Every profession, business, church, and discipline needed for a thriving community was contained within about a three-square mile area. During segregation in the 1950s, the only thing missing was air conditioning and a swimming pool. The original Carver Branch Library was on East Boulevard and became an educational haven for children. They could spend countless hours reading books while lying on the floor. Through these experiences, Coach Carl Stewart said that children could travel the world and explore the wonders of their imagination stimulated by books. And it was the perfect price…free. This photo is what the Carver Branch Library looked like in 2020. It is in no way the original structure enjoyed during the 1950s.

Page 4 Grandmother Gert

Pictured left to right: Gertrude "Gertie or Gert" Feast Baker, Jack Feast who was Gert's dad, Avis Delores Baker-White (Gert's daughter), and Simone Elizabeth Jefferson (a child cousin in the family). Gertie Feast Baker was my mother's (Avis Baker-White's) mom. Grandmother Gert made tea cakes which were almost like sugar cookies, but a little dryer and with a lemony taste. They were the cookie of choice at special occasions like a tea party. Lemonade was the preferred drink, too. I have fond memories of Grandmother Gert making dozens of those cookies by hand. Eating those cookies brings back waves of fond memories and carefree days as a child.

Page 5 A Chicken Shack Meal

The Chicken Shack was one of the original Black-owned businesses in South Baton Rouge. It began in 1935 by Thomas H. Delpit. It is still thriving over 85 years later operated by his son, Joseph A. Delpit Sr. (also known as Joe Delpit). Today there are several locations around the Baton Rouge area. It is definitely a hot spot for locals and a destination stop for visitors coming through Baton Rouge. Southern fried chicken, sweet potato pies, mustard greens, and Tuesday 2-piece specials are still very popular.

Page 5 Gilbert & Ezeria White's grandchildren

Back row left to right: Enovia White, Dana W. White, Robin White Clark (baby), Terry White, Ceola Rachel White and Cynthia White Criss (twin sisters). Seated left to right: Frank S. White, Lorraine E. White, DeQuilla Wayne White, and Trudy M. White. Sibling groups are 1) Dana, Trudy, and Robin, 2) Terry and Wayne, and 3) Frank with twin Enovia, Lorraine, and twins, Rachel and Cynthia. We were all on the porch at Ezeria and Gilbert White's house on South 18th Street in South Baton Rouge.

Page 6 Burdette White

Burdette L. White (my aunt) and her unnamed friend are near the corner of Government Street and Park Boulevard in the Garden District in South Baton Rouge. Across Government Street at that corner, it turns into South 19th Street. Burdette was a physical education teacher for many years in the West Baton Rouge Parish School System. In the 50's and 60's, Burdette worked across the river in Bachelor during the week and came home on weekends. Many lives were touched by her accomplishments, talents, and faithfulness to athletic sports such as basketball. She could call a serious game of basketball. She spent many years as a P.E. teacher and coach at Scotlandville and Capitol High Schools too in East Baton Rouge parish. She also worked for BREC which is our local parks and recreation organization. She was beloved as a giving and humorous individual. She was a person full of wit and a real deal frank talker. She

	was the mother of five children (Cynthia White, Ceola Rachel White, Frank Seth White, Enovia White, and Lorraine E. White).
Page 6 Gilly White's car	"Back in the day" people really dressed up. It was common to see people wearing what today in 2020 appears to be dressy clothes. Gilly, my father, worked as a pharmacist for Pool's Pharmacy and Food Town in North Baton Rouge before working at Schwegmann's in New Orleans in the 70's. He later worked for Katz and Bestoff (K & B) as its first Black pharmacist in Baton Rouge. This photo is my father, Gilbert "Gilly" A. White outside our former home at 1054 South 16th Street Baton Rouge, LA 70802. He had an air about himself that is captured in this photo. Gilly was always the life of any party. He always wore fedoras or Kangol hats on his head.
Page 7 Avis Baker-White	Minimum wage in 1953 was 75 cents/hour. About one-third of Blacks were unemployed or had unskilled jobs. Times were dire for most. Exceptional jobs would be positions in the chemical plant industry such as Standard Oil/ESSO, in hospital jobs as nurses or in the educational field as teachers. He worked with my grandmother's father, Jack Feast, at Standard Oil. My mother, Avis Baker-White, graduated with a Bachelor's degree in Education from Southern University. By the age of 19, she was teaching at McKinley High School in South Baton Rouge. South Baton Rouge called the general location of the school, "The Bottom." It was so named because there was a huge hill that you had to walk or drive down to get to the school. Attached is a postcard to my mom. It was representative of the kind of correspondence that was popular. I think the cost to mail a standard letter was 3 cents.
Page 7 1953 Bus	Independently owned Black bus companies such as the Blue Goose Bus and Jelly Bean were no longer operable. Leonard Brown was a family friend that lived next door to our house on Myrtle Walk. He owned buses. Since all Black-owned buses were declared illegal during this climate of segregation, he and other Black bus owners were prohibited from helping with the Baton Rouge Bus Boycott. Affordable mobility was now walking, taxis or using the Free Ride System. Few Blacks owned cars during these economically challenging and segregated times. This bus is an example of the model of bus that was typical in the 1950s. It is no longer operable, but is as an outdoor bus endorsed by Ms. Sadie Roberts-Joseph.
Page 8 Baton Rouge African American Museum	It was becoming increasingly tense and economically difficult for Blacks to manage a job when transportation was an obstacle every day due to segregation. The Baton Rouge Bus Boycott was almost inevitable. Few jobs. Increasing fares. Biased treatment. Walking and carpooling were the only peaceable options. This is a photo in 2020 of the Odell S. Williams Museum of African American History (renamed the Baton Rouge African American Museum in May 2019) founded by Sadie Roberts-Joseph. It displays and captures a wide array of African-American history for education and inspiration. Ms. Sadie was a beloved 75-year-old civil rights activist and educator cherished by the community. She served on countless organizations from the local to national level. Her tireless work and love for the community are enduring images that fuel her legacy's permanence. Her children, Dr. Angela R. Machen and Jason Roberts, treasure Ms. Sadie's life's work and honor her legacy.

THE BATON ROUGE BUS BOYCOTT

Page 8
Two boys on the front porch

Blacks were paying full fare, but only had access to the rear seats on the bus as they boarded. Even if seats were available in the front, Blacks had to start or "go to the back of the bus." Sitting on this porch step are Ronald Davidson and his older brother, Arthur Turner Davidson. Both boys would grow up to be well respected doctors with thriving practices. In this picture they represent the mood of the 1950s as they sit on the front porch of our grandparent's house (Gilbert and Ezeria Blanchard White).

Page 9
First two seats for Whites only

Prior to the Baton Rouge Bus Boycott, city buses were segregated. The bus did not have parallel seats from front to back on both sides of a center aisle. Instead, it had two long seats facing each other and parallel to the bus walls right behind the bus driver. Those seats faced each other and were reserved for Whites only. Look closely at the photo. See the bus driver's steering wheel, the driver's seat, a wheel well, and then the "White seat" next to the bus wall. The next seats turn 90 degrees and create a uniform pattern all the way to the back of the bus. During the 1950s, there would be a sign on the parallel seats at some point signifying the end of the Whites Only Section and the beginning of the "Colored Section."

Page 9
Finley's Drug Store

The proprietor, John L. Finley Jr., of Finley Pharmacy opened this first store in 1950 at 1388 Davis Avenue (now Dr. Martin Luther King Avenue) Mobile, AL. With his brother, James Finley, they opened up the second location in 1959. Eventually, six stores were opened representing the first Black-owned chain of drugstores in Alabama. Mr. Finley was a pharmacist who graduated from Xavier University in New Orleans, LA with my father, Gilbert "Gilly" A. White. Gilly was the first college graduate in his family. He was instrumental and helped finance the college education for his brother, Blanchard White, and two sisters, Burdette White and Genevieve White Davidson.

Finley was a big proponent of customer service. He insisted on having a clean sidewalk and clean windows every single day. When his son, Eric L. Finley, was about 8 years old, he was charged with the daily duty of sweeping that sidewalk. It was a matter of welcoming customers to the store. The Mobile, AL community in that area was much like that of South Baton Rouge at the same period of time in the 1950s. They too had a close-knit and thriving Black community. Mobile, AL had hat shops, theatres, barbers, doctors, and all types of businesses required for daily living. It would not be uncommon to see people well-dressed or even a man in a canary yellow suit!

Page 10
Three Men

(Left to right) Mann Shelvin, Gilbert White (my grandfather), and Gilbert A. White (my father). Gilbert A. White was a pharmacist for over 50 years. He was one of precious few Black pharmacists in Louisiana who had that badge of distinction. He was a graduate of Xavier University in New Orleans, LA.

Page 10
A beautiful car

Brothers (left to right): Ronald Davidson and Arthur Turner Davidson. These are the sons of Genevieve White Davidson. These boys are my first cousins. Their mom was my father's oldest sister. She was the first born in her family and my father was the 2nd born to Gilbert and Ezeria Blanchard White in August of 1923.

Page 11 Mount Zion	Mount Zion First Baptist Church was the largest Black church in Louisiana in the 1950s, pastored by Rev. T. J. Jemison. His father, Rev. David V. Jemison, was the president of the nation's largest and most prestigious Black organization, the National Baptist Convention, which had more than six million members. Rev. David V. Jemison was the pastor of Tabernacle Baptist Church in Selma, AL. The Baton Rouge Bus Boycott model of free rides coordinated by churches was used by Dr. Martin Luther King Jr. in 1956 for the Montgomery Bus Boycott. Raymond Scott was a Black tailor in South Baton Rouge and the Secretary for the United Defense League.
Page 11 McKinley High School Alumni Center	This building is the oldest African American High school building in the state of Louisiana. It was originally called the Hickory Street School in 1907 at a different site. It was relocated again in 1914 and named the Baton Rouge Colored School. Finally, on September 19, 1927 the school was relocated to Thomas H. Delpit Drive in Baton Rouge as McKinley High School. In February of 1992, the McKinley Alumni Association purchased the property at 1520 Thomas H. Delpit Drive B.R., LA 70802. McKinley Magnet High School is a diverse public school located on East McKinley Street in Baton Rouge, LA.
Page 12 Memorial Stadium	When the bus boycott meetings outran the capacity of local churches, BREC's Memorial Stadium became the new facility for mass gatherings and discussions. The stadium was very near South Baton Rouge and people could assemble there easily. This stadium has the capacity to seat 21,500 people. It was built in 1952. This photo was taken in 2020.
Page 12 George Butler, Willis V. Reed Sr., and T. Roosevelt Smith Sr.	Dr. George Butler was a pharmacist. The corner drug store where he worked was across the street from McKinley High School during the 1950s. The Ideal Drug Store no longer exists, but the property is now additional parking for the McKinley High School Alumni Center. Willis V. Reed Sr. owned and operated the Baton Rouge Post newspaper and was a lifelong community activist. He was founder and president of the First Ward Voters League. "T. Roosevelt Smith" was Theodore Roosevelt Smith Sr. He was the Executive Chairman of the Board of the United Defense League of which Rev. T. J. Jemison was President. That means Rev. T. J. Jemison reported to T. Roosevelt Smith Sr. In the 2nd photo are 4 generations after T. Roosevelt Smith Sr. From left to right: Brandon R. Smith (great-grandson), Theodore Roosevelt Smith Jr. (son), Renard A. Smith (grandson) and the baby, Brandon D. R. Smith (great-great-grandson).
Page 13 New St. John Baptist Church	Acie J. Belton was one of the most respected civil rights leaders in Louisiana and President of the Second Ward Voters League which was instrumental in getting Blacks registered to vote. Rev. E. Doyle Billoups was a giant in the community. He was a dynamic pastor of New St. John Baptist Church during the boycott time. He cared about people and was active politically. He became vice president of the National Baptist Convention USA. This photo is a 2020 picture of New St. John Baptist church. Adolph Wiggins Sr. worked at the post office in downtown Baton Rouge and for the postal union. Eight people were inducted into the Louisiana Black History Hall of Fame on June 20, 1992 for their involvement in the Baton Rouge Bus Boycott. They

were as follows: Rev. T. J. Jemison, Willis V. Reed Sr., Dr. George Butler, Adolph Wiggins Sr., Rev. E. Doyle Billoups, Acie J. Belton, T. Roosevelt Smith Sr., and Raymond Scott.

Page 13 Desselle Funeral & Insurance	In 1948, Adam D. Desselle founded a funeral home that was centrally located in South Baton Rouge. Desselle also established Desselle's Life Insurance Company. The funeral home still exists today on Eddie Robinson Sr. Drive in Baton Rouge. During the bus boycott, funeral home vehicles were used to provide free rides around the city.
Page 14 Free Ride System	People who owned cars would either drive their cars in the shuttle Free Ride System, help neighbors around them or allow someone else to drive their car in the bus boycott effort. This photo was taken at our family home on the corner of South 16th Street on Myrtle Walk (aka Myrtle Street) in South Baton Rouge. My parents (Avis Baker-White and Gilbert "Gilly" A. White) are featured in the center of this photo.
Page 14 Old State Capitol	It was on the side street just outside of the Old State Capitol where many boycott participants loaded and unloaded from cars and taxis in the Free Ride System. There was an ongoing shift of vehicles that would provide transportation for participants beginning early in the morning and ending late in the afternoon. No questions asked. This strategy paired with droves of people walking would ultimately impact the income generated by the segregated public city buses. It was an economic nightmare for the city bus system. The city bus system would not be able to survive without the income generated by the Black riders.
Page 15 A Typical Day in 1953	This is a scene from Myrtle Walk in South Baton Rouge near the corner of South 16th Street. Gilbert "Gilly" A. White holds his son, Dana W. White, who was born in 1953. The streets are lined with the typical shotgun houses in rows on the right and classic 1950s cars.
Page 15 Stately Gentleman	This was probably a Sunday. Gilbert White (my grandfather) was a painter. (He had no middle name.) When not in his painter's pants, he was a dapper dresser on Sunday. Though not formally educated and probably illiterate, he managed to instill a value in his four children to pursue and attain a college education before he died in July of 1987. The educational success of Gilbert White's children changed the educational and economic power of all of the grandchildren. The grandchildren are veterans, doctors, dentists, judges, attorneys, teachers, entrepreneurs, and other occupations.
Page 16 Emergency Ordinance 251	This text box represents an abbreviation of Ordinance 251. It was "necessary that the Council now adopt a suitable ordinance regulating the seating of passengers on buses for hire within the City of Baton Rouge and an emergency, within the meaning of Section 2.12 of the Plan of Government exists, requiring that such ordinance be adopted without the necessity of a public hearing…."
Page 16 Perkins Road Elementary	Everything was segregated. It was the law. The White bus drivers resented the fact that they could not serve White passengers only. They had to serve Black passengers too. Perkins Road Elementary school served only Black students in South Baton Rouge due to segregation. This school was across the street from my Grandmother

	Gert's red brick house on South 16th Street at Bynum Street. Twin sisters (Rachel White on the left and Cynthia White) attended school here. The building was demolished and years later Wonderland Headstart was built on the same site.
Page 17 A White seat	This is a photo of one of the two front seats for Whites only. It could seat about 3 adults. To the right of the seat, you see the wheel well. Farther to the right after that would be the bus driver's seat. Left of this seat out of the photo would be where the seats would change directions 90 degrees and face the front of the bus.
Page 17 The middle seats for all & This book's cover photo	Once the Emergency Ordinance 251 was passed and enforced, it represented at least a compromise in the seating of passengers. Now there were only two seats in the front which were only for Whites and a back seat (or a split seat) at the very back of the bus which was for Blacks. The middle seats were available to all. Three seats were "color coded" and the rest were up for grabs within the constraints of the emergency ordinance. This photo shows five outstanding community leaders. Those in the front row (left to right) are Attorney Johnnie A. Jones Sr. and Martha White. Martha White was the Black housekeeper who boarded the segregated city bus one morning in June. The only available seat left was in the "Whites Only" section directly behind the bus driver and that's where she sat. She was truly a catalyst for the beginning of the Baton Rouge Bus Boycott. In 1953, Attorney Johnnie A. Jones Sr. was the lead attorney on the Baton Rouge Bus Boycott case. Standing in the back row of the photo are three individuals. They are (from left to right) Marjorie Green, Russell L. Kelly Sr. and Sadie Roberts-Joseph. Marjorie Green and Russell L. Kelly Sr. remain active politically. They continue to show civil rights activism and visibility whenever called. They are living examples of knowing and preserving our Black history.
Page 18 The Compromise	It was during June of 1953 when Blacks formed the United Defense League (UDL) and organized the Baton Rouge Bus Boycott. A compromise with the Baton Rouge City Council and UDL was met after one week. The first two rows on each bus would be reserved for White passengers. Blacks could choose to sit anywhere after that. The Free Ride System could begin to disband. Segregation was still alive, but this was the emergency remedy for the situation in Baton Rouge. Dr. Martin Luther King Jr. collaborated and consulted with Rev. T. J. Jemison regarding the Free Ride System held during the Baton Rouge Bus Boycott. Dr. Martin Luther King Jr. was the first president of the Montgomery Improvement Association. This organization organized the Montgomery Bus Boycott of 1955. Interestingly enough, Rev. Jemison's dad was a pastor in Selma, AL just 54 miles from Montgomery, AL. In this photo (standing on the far left) is my Aunt Genevieve White Davidson. She is my dad's sister.
Page 19 Reflecting Pool Downtown BR Riverfront	Resilience and resolve still empower the resident Blacks of South Baton Rouge. Education, economic power, voting, and political activism are creating solutions for a brighter future. The community of Blacks are involved in almost every facet of the community from the mayor-president's office to the courthouse to the university.

Page 19 Memorial Bench	"On a bench by the road" symbolizes a time of stillness and purpose on a pathway to implementing a plan. Stillness does not mean idleness. It takes quietness to hear the voice of God speaking into your spirit and to know what to do with what is in your hands. God gives us potential. It is up to us to live a life to fulfill our purpose and capture that potential. He will give us light for each step of the journey. What mark will you leave on the world? (Just don't let it be a question mark.) Holy Spirit lead us.
Page 20 The Baker Family Legacy	Learn and know what was done before you arrived on the scene. Do research. Ask questions. Understand and position yourself for holding on to the positive steps made by others who have come before you. Record it and leave a legacy that impacts other people. Celebrate each victory. Photo (left to right back row): Gloria Dean Gardere Gray Monroe Hooper, George Walter Baker Sr. (great uncle), Ruby Taylor Harris, Joseph Francis Baker (great uncle), William Alvin Baker (grandfather), and Avis Baker-White (mother). Sitting in chairs left to right: Christine Bell Dennis, Mary "Mama" Francis Baker (great-grandmother), George "Papa" Harold Baker (great-grandfather), Florence Jane Baker Benjamin, and Lillian Baker Gardere. Children sitting left to right: George Walter Baker, Jr., Margaret Hunter (Benjamin), Thearon Alvin Baker, Marilyn Baker Smith Guy, and Dalton Chaney. As of the printing of this book in 2020, my mom is one of the oldest living persons on the Baker side of the family. She is 93 years-old and the oldest living "Baker"! The people who are still living on the first row are in their 70s. This is my mom's family. Her first cousin was Dr. Ruby Taylor Harris who was a notable educator that died at 100 years-old in 2016. Ruby's mom (Mary Elizabeth Baker) died July 27, 1927. My grandfather, William Alvin Baker, and his siblings inherited over 400 acres off of Perkins Road in Baton Rouge.
Page 20 Freedom Bell	Although the palpable effects of Jim Crow laws and segregation were (and are) present, the Baton Rouge Bus Boycott presented a model to other cities that followed. Even Dr. Martin Luther King Jr. consulted with local leaders such as Rev. T. J. Jemison to understand the model and methods used in the first bus boycott in the South. This photo was taken in New Orleans at the Whitney Plantation.
Page 22 Acie J. Belton	Acie J. Belton – He was the founder of the Second Ward Voters League. At the time, Scotlandville was an independent and rural community. As a community leader in Scotlandville, there was little to no Black elected officials and politicians. Belton would speak with the White candidates and create a ballot for distribution to the Black community of candidates who supported their goals. Later, Belton was instrumental in challenging the law for Scotlandville to be added to the city of Baton Rouge. At all times, Belton worked to overcome the disenfranchisement of the Black worker.
Page 23 Rev. E. Doyle Billoups	Rev. E. Doyle Billoups – He was Vice President-At-Large of the National Baptist Convention. This organization boasted a membership of over six million members across the nation. It was a powerful force and network with unifying ties of faith and focus for the Black community leaders. He was also president of the Fourth District Baptist Association that assisted with the Baton Rouge Bus Boycott.

Page 24 Dr. George A. Butler	Dr. George Butler – He was a pharmacist in the South Baton Rouge community. He worked at the Ideal Drug Store at the corner across from the McKinley High School (now the Alumni Center). He and his brother, Dr. Leo S. Butler, built the Butler Building on East Boulevard. It housed Black-owned business and a modern medical office too. It has since been demolished. Their family home at 963 Terrace Street was used as a site to host Black political figures, visiting dignitaries, community action groups, sororities and fraternities throughout the 40s and 50s. Due to the lack of public facilities for people of color, this home became a repository for the Black community in South Baton Rouge. At one point, a young piano prodigy named Philippa Schuyler held an impromptu concert there. She is the daughter of the noted publisher named George Schuyler.
Page 25 Judge Lewis S. Doherty III	Judge Lewis S. Doherty III – He was a distinguished attorney and judge whose moral and ethical convictions about equality of races was demonstrated in his work. His values and stance were generally considered in favor of civil rights. He was one of the White members of the Baton Rouge City Council in 1953 when the Emergency Ordinance 251 was established to end the Baton Rouge Bus Boycott.
Page 26 Hazel Lucille Johnson Freeman	Hazel Lucille Johnson Freeman – Ms. Freeman was a member of Mount Zion Baptist Church which had the largest Black membership of Black churches in Louisiana at the time. She and Reverend T. J. Jemison arrived at the scene when Martha White refused to comply with the White bus driver's requests on a segregated bus. She was also the secretary to Gardner C. Taylor, the former pastor of Mount Zion Baptist Church before Rev. T. J. Jemison.
Page 27 Rev. T. J. Jemison	Rev. T. J. Jemison – Pastor of Mount Zion Baptist Church during the boycott. Instrumental in selecting the attorney for the bus boycott case. Collaborated with Martin Luther King Jr. about the first successful boycott in the nation. Shared the blueprint for Free Ride System organized by a church group. My grandfather was the treasurer of Mount Zion Baptist church. The first Sunday dinner with Rev. T. J. Jemison was installed as pastor of Mount Zion Baptist Church in Baton Rouge was at William Alvin Baker's house. William Alvin Baker was my maternal grandfather.
Page 28 Attorney Johnnie A. Jones Sr.	Attorney Johnnie A. Jones Sr. – He was the lead attorney who pursued legal changes against segregation on the public buses in Baton Rouge. He was only 15 days out of law school when he accepted the case.
Page 29 Sadie Roberts-Joseph	Sadie Roberts-Joseph –Ms. Sadie, as she was affectionately called, boasted a legacy of activism, community service works, and collaborations to unify people of all races. This beloved community icon was the curator responsible for the Odell S. Williams Museum in Baton Rouge, LA. This museum holds artifacts and treasures of our Black American History.

Page 30 Willis V. Reed Sr.	Willis V. Reed Sr. – By 1953, Mr. Reed help found the First Ward Voters League. This group influenced voting in Baton Rouge politics. He spoke out for changes in the Black community and help influence voting blocks. He was known for being the owner and operator of the Baton Rouge Post, a Black community newspaper.
Page 31 Raymond Scott	Raymond Scott – The lead organization for the Baton Rouge Bus Boycott was the United Defense League. Raymond Scott was the secretary of that organization. Surely, he knew the status of events and understood the importance of the effort. During the 1950s, Scott's Tailor was the only place in the Black community of South Baton Rouge where men could get tuxedos and formal wear. A family friend of ours (Ed Pratt) recalls that Raymond Scott was a good guy behind the scenes. He had one of the nicer homes in the community on the corner of East Boulevard and Education Street. He remembers him as being referred to as Scott, The Tailor.
Page 32 T. Roosevelt Smith Sr.	T. Roosevelt Smith Sr. - Mr. Smith was President of the Colored Union at Standard Oil/ESSO (now ExxonMobil) and instrumental in the desegregation of that facility. He was a founding member of the Purple Circle Social Club and reported to be the first Black bailiff for the 19th Judicial District. His name continues to command respect and acknowledgment as a Black leader. He was called Prexy which was short for president. He earned this nickname due to the fact that he held the title in many respectable organizations of influence and importance to the Black community.
Page 33 Horatio C. Thompson	Horatio C. Thompson – He was the first Black businessman in Baton Rouge to own gas station franchises and provided gasoline to boycott drivers at his wholesale cost. Mr. Thompson was a founder and charter member of Alpha Sigma Chapter of Kappa Alpha Psi Fraternity, Inc. Over his lifespan he was a member and held offices in over 50 prestigious organizations. His daughters are Phyllis White and Paula Honore.
Page 34 Martha White	Martha White – She is truly the hidden figure in the Baton Rouge Bus Boycott history. She was the 23-year-old housekeeper who defied the segregation law on a public Baton Rouge city bus. Her actions led to the Baton Rouge Bus Boycott, the first successful bus boycott in the nation. The model of the Free Ride System was later used by Dr. Martin Luther King Jr. for the successful boycott in Montgomery, Alabama. Martha White is not related to the author of this book as far as I know.
Page 35 Adolph Wiggins Sr.	Adolph Wiggins Sr. – J. W. Vaughn remembers that Adolph Wiggins Sr. was a magnificent man. He was a long-time member of Alpha Phi Alpha Fraternity on North Foster Drive. It was Adolph who helped acquire the building and maintain it. Mr. Vaughn recalls that Adolph and Sister Wiggins were a very close couple. He was known to be a great humanitarian who was very blessed. Adolph simply loved helping people. He loved traveling and was a devout Catholic person who attended mass at St. Joseph's Cathedral.

www.ingramcontent.com/pod-product-compliance
Lightning Source LLC
Chambersburg PA
CBHW081330040426

42453CB00013B/2362